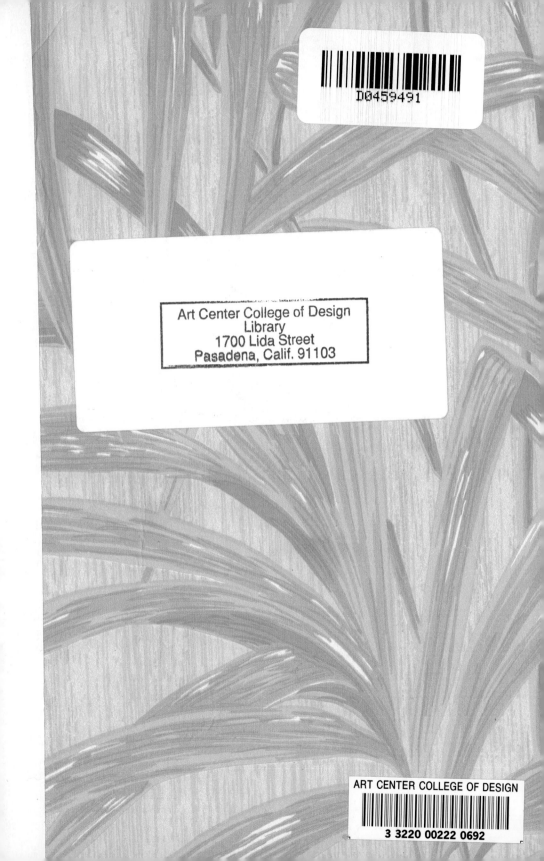

WALLCOVERINGS

from the F. Schumacher & Co. Collections

Applying
the Language
of Color and Pattern

Also published by Universe:

Great American Houses and Gardens
by Chuck Fischer
ISBN: 0-7893-0798-7

New Loft Living: Arranging Your Space
by Elizabeth Wilhide
ISBN: 0-7893-0818-5

1000 Practical Ideas for Home Decoration
by Anna Ventura
ISBN: 0-7893-0666-2

First published in the United States of America in 2003
by UNIVERSE PUBLISHING
A Division of Rizzoli International Publications, Inc.
300 Park Avenue South
New York, NY 10010

2003 2004 2005 2006 2007 / 10 9 8 7 6 5 4 3 2 1

Printed in Hong Kong

ISBN: 0-7893-0851-7

Library of Congress Control Number: 2002110927

Designer: Lionize, Inc. New York, NY
Universe editor: Jessica Fuller

WALLCOVERINGS

from the F. Schumacher & Co. Collections

Applying
the Language
of Color and Pattern

Chuck Fischer

UNIVERSE

TABLE OF CONTENTS

FOREWORD

Chuck Fischer's *Wallcoverings : Applying the Language of Color and Pattern* is a feast of color and pattern to delight the eye and stir the imagination.

For over one hundred years, the most beautiful houses in America—from the White House to the Metropolitan Opera House—have been graced with the high quality and classic design of fabric and wall-coverings from Schumacher. The material that Chuck has selected from the archives of F. Schumacher & Co. is extraordinarily rich and varied—a collection that will not only delight, but will also bring varied elements of design into strong focus for a wide audience.

Chuck Fischer's own background as an artist and decorative painter is well expressed in this charming and handsome book—a book that will serve its audience well as teacher and as guide.

As a designer, my goal is to help clients realize more than they thought possible within the framework of their own tastes. Chuck worked with me at the beginning of his career, and it's exciting for me to see—for the first time in book form—an encapsulation of his talent and imagination that readers can readily access when considering changes in their own office and living environments. With *Wallcoverings*, Chuck revels in two of my favorite things : a sustained sense of tradition and an inexhaustible curiosity for the new.

—Albert Hadley
New York, 2002

INTRODUCTION

"White walls, unrelieved by any color, are relics of barbarism and are almost a thing of the past."
— *Picturesque California Homes*, 1885

The joy of living with color and pattern is the essence of my design philosophy, and it is the inspiration for this collection of exquisite wallcoverings. Color and pattern are both powerful visual and emotional decorating tools. I hope this book gives new insight and inspiration for making color and pattern choices.

In 1889, Frederick Schumacher founded F. Schumacher & Co., launching an enterprise that has become the gold standard in wallcovering and textile design. The company Mr. Schumacher established over a century ago has made a distinguished contribution to some of America's finest interiors, including the White House, the Waldorf-Astoria Hotel, and Cornelius Vanderbilt's home, the Breakers.

My association with F. Schumacher & Co. began a few years ago when signature designs of mine were first introduced in the fall 2001 collections. I continue to introduce new designs based on my years spent creating one-of-a-kind hand-painted murals in some of the finest residences in the world. I was attracted to F. Schumacher & Co. because it has been at the forefront of presenting exciting new colors and trends in design. At the same time it has maintained the tradition of a classic to-the-trade institution whose wallcoverings and textiles have become a part of American decorative history.

How to Use This Book

Color has a profound influence on our lives. Reviewing some basic color theory will help you effectively use color to create the appropriate mood for a room. There are three primary colors: red, yellow, and blue. When two of these colors are mixed together they create one of the three secondary colors: orange (red and yellow), green (blue and yellow), and violet (red and blue). These colors are often arranged on a wheel with the six tertiary colors between them: red-orange, yellow-orange, yellow-green, blue-green, blue-violet, and red-violet. You will notice on a color wheel that the red, orange, and yellow half of the wheel feels warm and appears to come forward visually. The green, blue, and violet hues feel cool and appear to recede. This basic observation is important to consider when planning the color scheme of a room.

It is also important to consider ideas about hues and color combination. Selecting any hue and its opposite color on the wheel is called a complementary (or contrasting) color combination. When tints or tones of the same color are used throughout a room, the scheme is called monochromatic.

The most striking feature of this book is that it provides the opportunity to observe, in full scale, hundreds of designs—from traditional patterns inspired by historical looks to fresh, contemporary designs—within one sourcebook. Notice how one color feels different when used with other colors or a neutral tone. To illustrate the themes inspired while perusing thousands of samples of wallcoverings for this book, I chose the following layouts with great care. Whether through color, pattern, subject matter, or a combination of all three design elements, I wanted to demonstrate here how seemingly unrelated designs often share a common theme.

This myriad assortment of wallcovering designs is organized by the principles of the color wheel. Each chapter focuses on one of the twelve colors of the color wheel and begins with a lively rendering of a room, accompanied by some examples of how to use the color. Normally I paint finely detailed watercolor room renderings; for this book, I created collages out of fragments of wallpaper that are featured throughout this book. For example, the Violet chapter opener on page 232 combines five patterns that demonstrate my ideas about combining varying patterns in shades of violet and complementing them with neutral accents.

Additionally, each color section is arranged dark to light, with an identifying page number (and letter where, in some instances, more than one pattern appears on a spread) in order to cross-reference each design in the index. The index provides the title of the wallcovering, the colorway, the name of the collection, and a brief description of the design and/or example of how it can be used in decorating your home. I have also compiled thoughts about wallcoverings, color, and pattern from some of America's most talented decorators and design editors, which run throughout the index.

I hope the papers and ideas featured in *Wallcoverings* will spark your design interest and inspire you to live and decorate with color and pattern.

—Chuck Fischer
New York, 2002

RED evokes passion.

From soft pink flowers to fiery sunsets, red is a powerful color that has a warm and pleasing effect. A red room by day is beautiful and at night the glow of a red room enhances the complexion of everyone in the room. Red is a strong primary color—I have a red wallpapered entrance hall that is the perfect introduction to my home.

The tradition of "making an entrance" on red carpet dates back to ancient Chinese matrimonial customs. Cinnabar (the mineral source of vermilion) was the base for the original Imperial Red and prohibitively expensive, therefore available only to the nobility. Fortunately, in the thirteenth century a chemical formula for red was developed that popularized its use in domestic decoration, a tradition that continues to this day.

Red is such a sensual color, so full of life; surrounding oneself in a red room can be very energizing and stimulating. Using color in interior design is always very personal, so if a clear red is too overpowering for your taste, choose a softer red in the pink end of the spectrum. But always remember: red is a color that insists on being noticed.

The walls—Sutton Strie: Garnet (shown on page 18); In the mirror—Gracie Stripe: Raspberry, which also forms the backdrop for the book cover (pages 189 and 229)

14A 14B

17A

17B

18A   18B

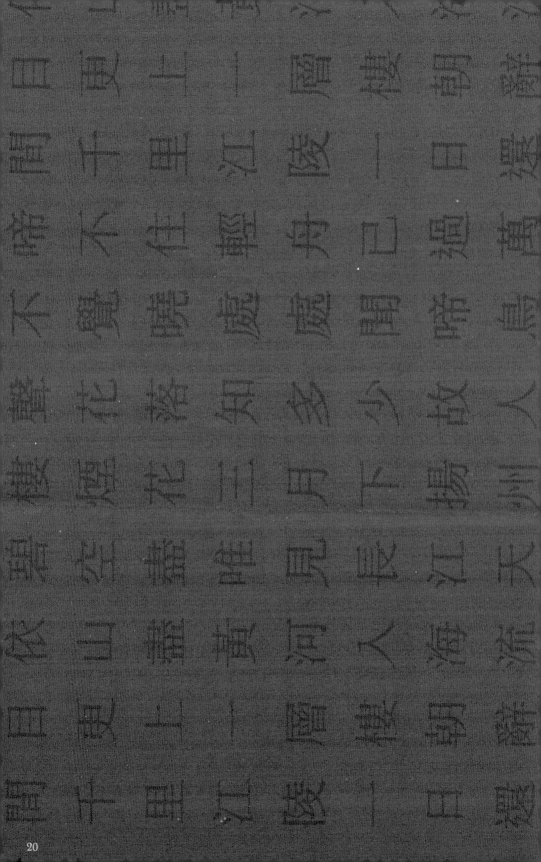

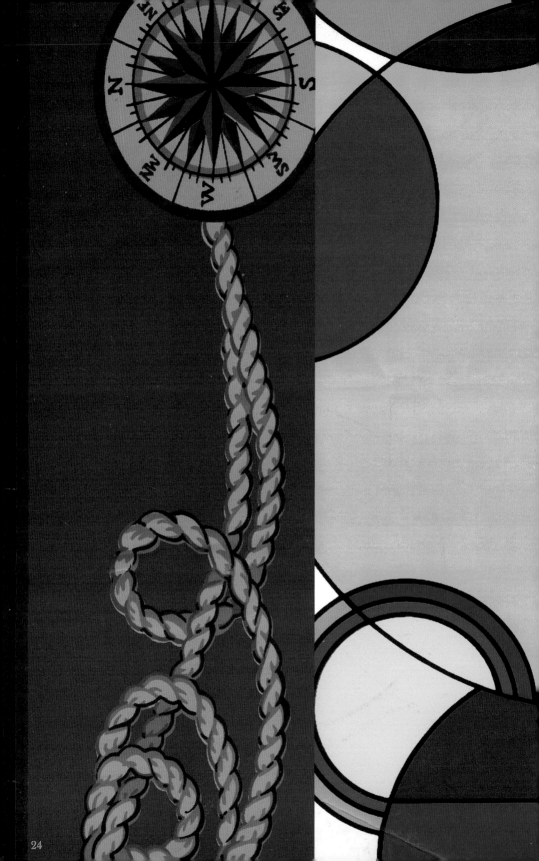

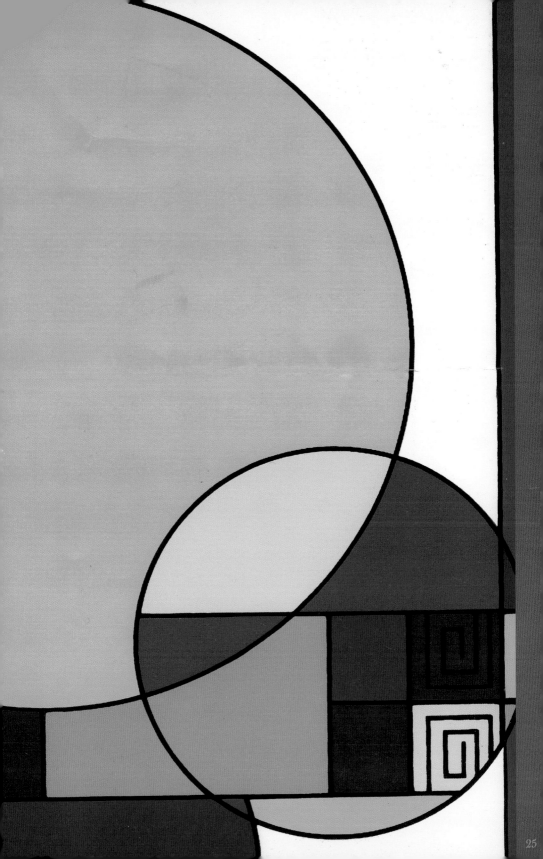

28A

28B

33B

38A

38B

42A 42B

buckle. Beware of little expences

eak, will sink a great ship.

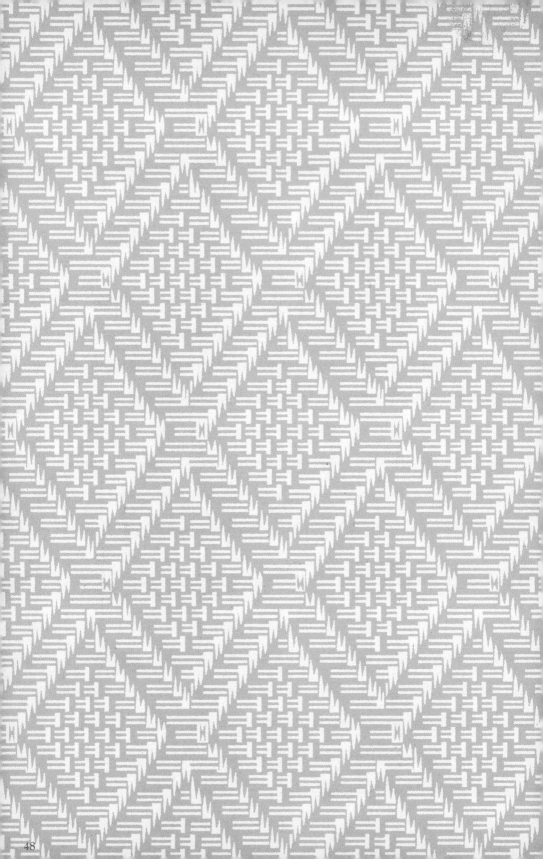

RED-
ORANGE

evokes warmth.

Red-orange has a casual elegance. From the textured skin of a tangerine to the polished smoothness of the inside of a conch shell, wallcovering shades of red-orange bring the outdoors to interiors. I think of summer bonfires, breathtaking autumn leaves, and winter sunsets. Norse mythology relates how animals with red-orange coloring—such as the fox, robin, and squirrel—were the god Thor's favorite creatures because of their red-orange color. Shades in red-orange's vivid, yet earthly palette are perfectly suited for any room in which you want to create a homey atmosphere full of warmth.

The lighter shades of red-orange can effectively be used to create a sophisticated dining room or luxurious bedroom. Sitting in a dining room with coral-colored walls, in the glow of red-orange candlelight reflecting off crystal and gold-rimmed china with accents of aqua, sets the perfect mood for stimulating conversation and good cheer.

The curtains—Alcott Plaid: Coral (pages 60–61); Floorboards—Mary Rose Stripe: Peach (pages 76–77); Rug—Akita: Oatmeal (pages 278–279); Outdoors—Spring Woods: Green on White (page 173)

52A   52B

54A

54B

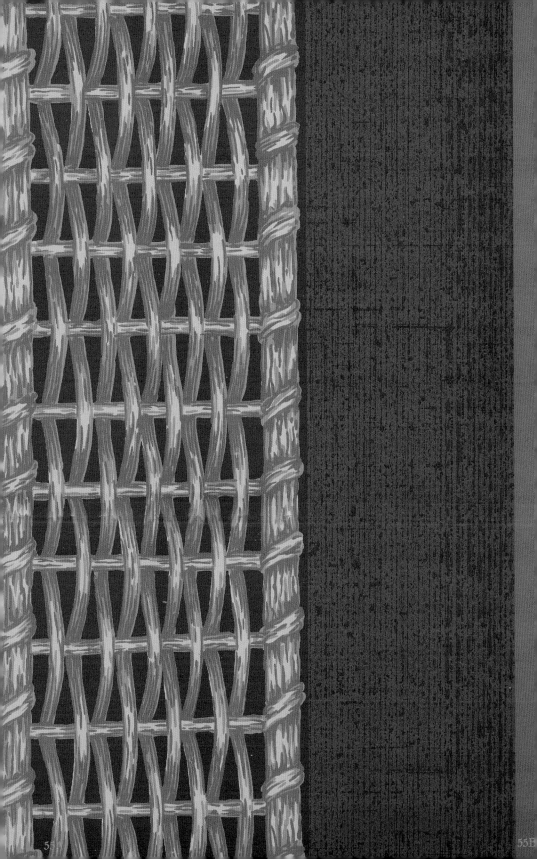

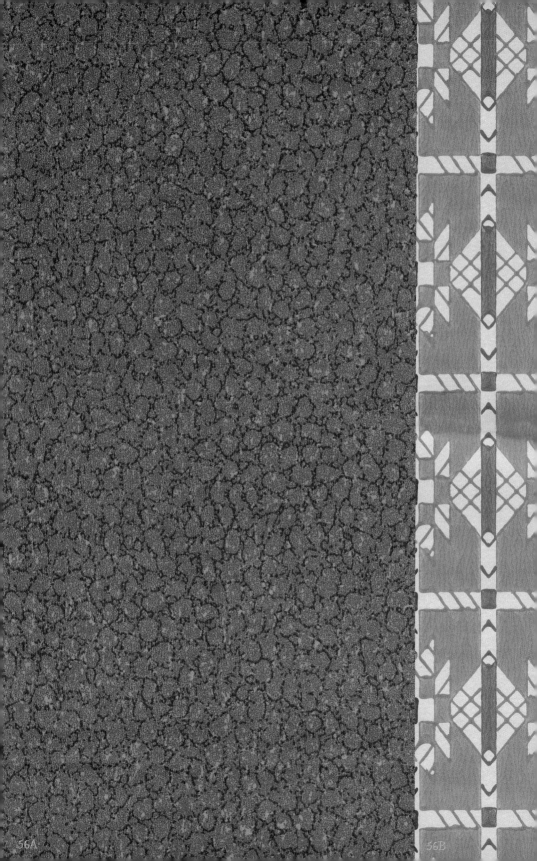

59

60A

60B

62B

ORANGE

is vibrant.

Orange is a youthful color that imparts sophistication and energy when used properly. Orange and sky-blue, a color scheme so beautiful in nature, is a natural combination for the home.

Not everyone can live with an abundance of vibrant orange, so changing the hue by adding some creamy white brings out the softer side of orange. Orange, salmon, and apricot are just a few words that embody the sensual pleasure of orange.

If you think about it, the orange itself has the energy of yellow and the passion of red; it is supported by a solid gray-brown branch; and it is accented with shoots of green leaves. This has the makings of a beautiful color scheme. A rich brown wood floor, your favorite shade of orange on the wall, accents of green, a cloud-white painted cornice, and a blue ceiling results in a striking look; the color combination evokes a youth and vibrancy that never goes out of fashion.

The walls—Indienne Stripe: Sage Green (page 77); the wainscoting—Linares Strie: Coral and Green (pages 76–77); the stairway—Leopard skin: Champagne (page 284); the carpet—Ningbo Sisal: Hunter (page 150); the rug—Indienne Border: Sage Green (page 76); the ceiling and artwork—Petits Elephants: Ivory (page 284)

Orange

and

74A

74B

76A

76B

76C

79A

79B

YELLOW-ORANGE

is energizing.

The warmth of yellow and the juiciness of orange combine to create a youthful, energetic color—a great color for a kitchen or family room and one that works particularly well in a children's playroom. The juggling jester on the harlequin background (page 91) illustrates how to use this color perfectly. The design is active and amusing, and full of motion and youth. The color combination demonstrates how complementary shades of blue used with accents of red-orange and yellow-green work so well together.

The ceiling—Twinkle, Twinkle: Aqua and Yellow (page 119); the wall—Jake's Jester: Yellow (page 91); the duvet—Ruth Audley Rose: Fuchsia and Yellow (page 83); the bedskirt—Stars n' Stripes: Yellow (pages 85–86); the floor and curtains—Taylor's Toss: Yellow (pages 116–117)

83A

83B

94

98A

98B

YELLOW

is illuminating.

Like the brightest star in the sky, yellow is the most illuminating primary color. Many of the most radiant and memorable rooms in the past century have been yellow: Nancy Lancaster's butter-yellow bedroom or Mario Buatta's classic East Side, New York City, living room.

There's no need to question why so many people have such a positive reaction to the color yellow. After all, it is the color of gold, butter, and ripe lemons.

Artists have been using yellow ochre—a natural pigment—for centuries. It wasn't until the nineteenth century when such new pigments as cadmium and chrome yellow were discovered that artists were able to use significantly more brilliant yellows. Van Gogh—whose favorite color in his palette was yellow—segued from using brownish yellow ochre in his earlier paintings into bright yellows to represent the sun of the south of France for his final paintings.

Yellow is a naturally refreshing and reflective color that works well in making it seem as if a room is constantly illuminated by the sun. Whether you are partial to golden honey tones or a sunny lemon yellow, the room you wallpaper in yellow will appear brighter and make a cheerful impression.

The walls—Strathmore Texture: Topaz (page 108); the screen—Bamboo Fret: Lacquer (page 27); the sofas—Linleigh Stripe: Sunflower (page 113); the rug—Taki Bamboo: Yellow (page 126)

107A

107B

108A   108B

112B

114 B

118A

118B

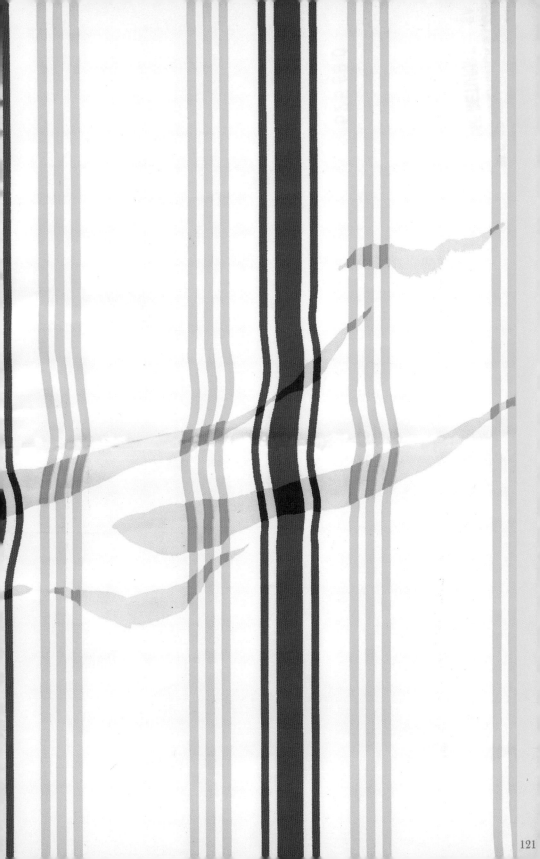

122A

122B

124A   124B

125A

125B

YELLOW-GREEN is fresh.

All colors look terrific when combined with yellow-green. I often see color combinations that exist in nature that would be perfect in my home. Looking to the shades of yellow-greens in late spring/early summer and the brilliant colors of flowers blooming en masse can be a great tool for creating a color scheme for a room.

Yellow-green is such a prominent color in nature; therefore, it is not surprising that many of the wallpapers in this section illustrate subjects from nature. Choose a yellow-green wallpaper for the background of any room and combine it with your favorite color from the garden. Visualize the growth of a new leaf and the spirit of soaking in the yellow lights of the sun. It is easy to feel that freshness every time you enter a room designed in yellow-green.

The carpet—Leopard Skin: Green (page 135); the walls and bed-skirt—La Grande: Sage (page 136); the duvet—Linwood Strie: Yellow (page 113)

139A

139B

143A

143B

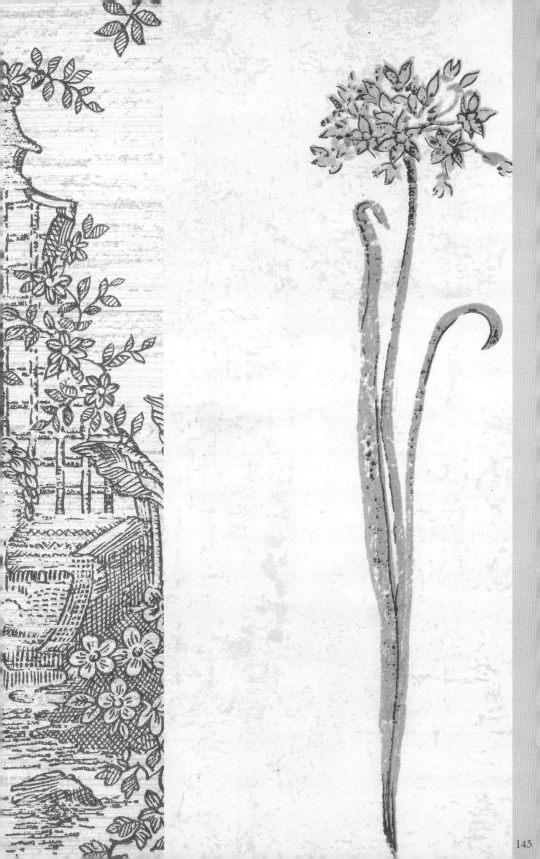

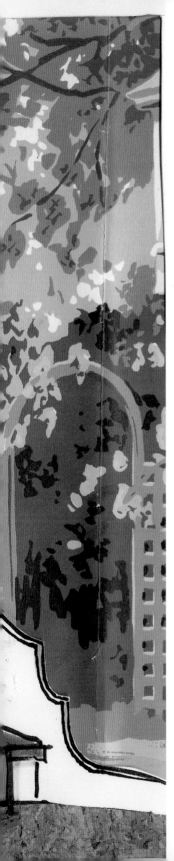

GREEN

is soothing.

Green is practically considered a neutral for many designers, including myself. A deep green painted on a floor or trellis covered in foliage on a screened porch can be very calming. Many people take walks in a leafy green forest to relax. That same comfort zone can be created at home by surrounding yourself with green, accented with any other color of the wheel, in a room. A lush forest in full leaf on a summer day is a cool sanctuary; a green room—whether it is your library, living room, bedroom, or dining room—can be a similar sanctuary in your home.

The walls—Spring Woods: Green on White (page 173); the stairs—Blenheim Damask: Green (pages 156–157); the flooring—Damask Arabesque Cork (pages 270–271); the rug and trim—Dianthus: Green and Fox Hound Border: Green (pages 152 and 155)

150A

150B

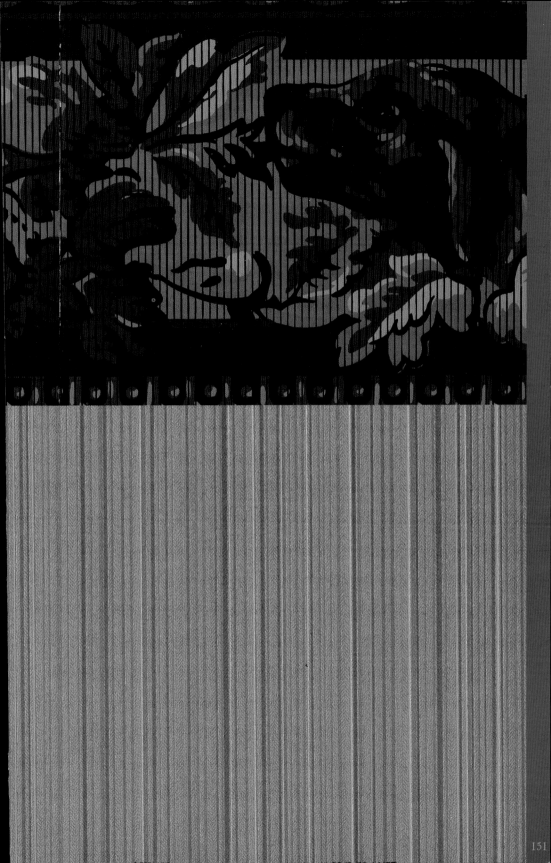

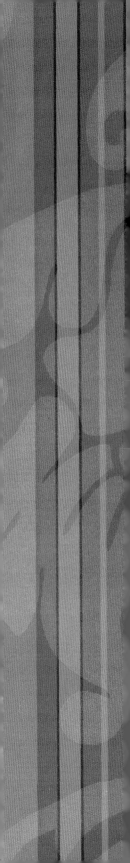

160 A

160 B

166

BLUE-GREEN

is cool.

Blue-greens are my favorite colors. Blue-green is the color of the Caribbean sea and the color of a Tiffany's box with an exciting surprise inside. Blue-green in a room is both vibrant and calming, very much the qualities of water. If you dream of the peacefulness of a deserted island surrounded by crystal clear blue-green water, the exotic foliage in a lush tropical garden, or simply a swimming pool in the backyard, a room full of blue-green is for you. Use a lot of the color on the walls and ceiling, paint the trim a sandy beige, hang a border to surround the space and you've created a pleasing environment bordering on the exotic.

I'll never forget the Parish-Hadley blue-green walls in the entrance hall at their Fifty-sixth Street offices in New York: uplifting, exotic, sophisticated, and daring like the feathers of a rare tropical bird. Add some reflective mirror, throw in some bright red-orange as an accent and you've got an inspired color combination for your favorite room.

Another slightly tamer combination is blue-green with yellow and terra-cotta. A yellow stucco house with dark green shutters and a terra-cotta tile room overlooking a turquoise sea results in a sensational inspiration for a color combination for any interior.

The walls—Ahmedabad Stripe: Aqua (page 189); the entranceway—Rosa di Sardinia: Document Aqua (page 186); the carpet—Tropique Border: Orange and Chocolate (pages 178–179)

181A

181B

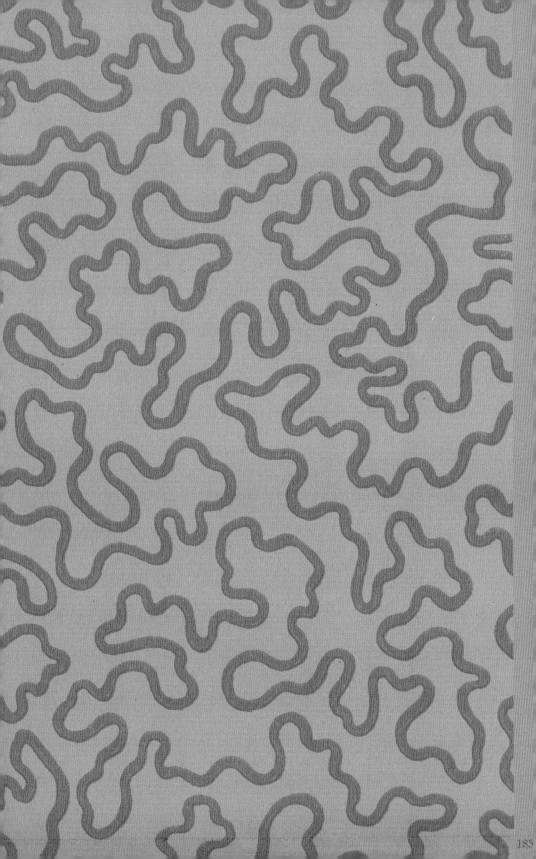

188B

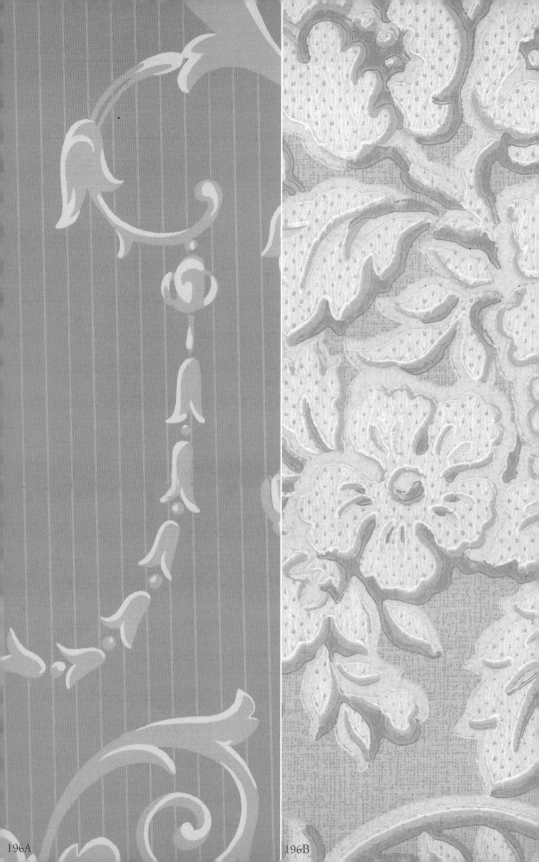

196A

196B

197A

197B

BLUE is classic.

Like a navy-blue blazer hanging in the closet, a blue room is dependable, smart-looking, and always appropriate. Historically, blue flowers were a very popular motif in nineteenth-century Romantic poetry; the Romantic poets believed visualizing blue could evoke a dreamlike state and a feeling of serenity and security.

Today, blue is certainly America's favorite color, and you can't go wrong when decorating with it. I think of dark blues as a nocturnal color, dreamy and full of depth. Whether blue is the deep shades of water reflecting a full moon or the blue-black of a clear night sky filled with stars, many shades of blue can be effectively combined in any room.

Some of the most successful rooms use lots of blue and white together. Find inspiration in antique Chinese porcelain, your favorite *toile de Jouy* or the many juxtapositions of blue and white at the yacht club. With blue you can create a crisp, contemporary look or the look of lived-in comfort, like a favorite pair of blue jeans.

Whatever blue you choose, it is bound to become a classic. Be confident that your room is cool, comfortable, and as distinguished as that navy-blue blazer.

The walls and window treatments—Sea Island Stripe: Aqua (page 209); the wainscoting, armoire, bed skirt, and throw rug—Palmettes de Cachemire and Border: Navy (pages 204–205); the bedspread and roll—Aurora Borealis: Navy (pages 199–200); the ceiling—Stencil Leaf Blue (page 208); the border—Ornamental Volute Border: Blue on White (page 210); the wall hanging and lamps—Royal Crowns: Royal Blue and Gold (page 200)

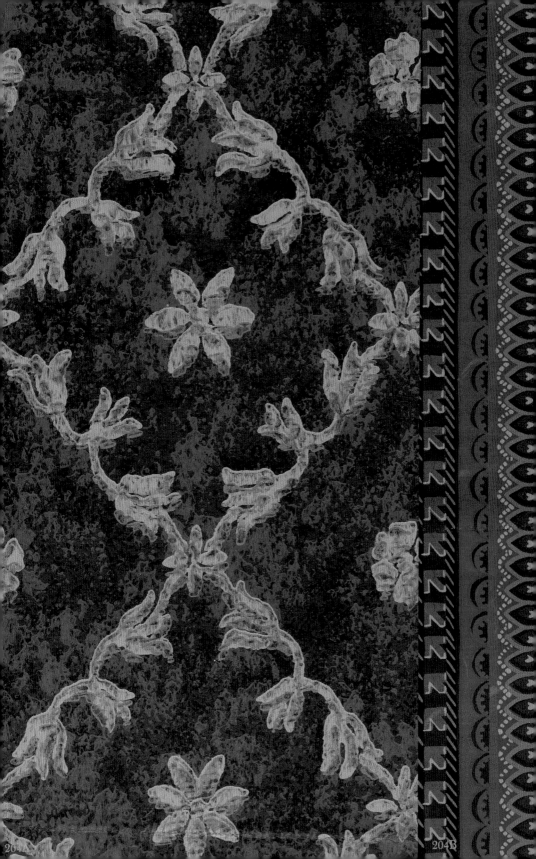

208A

208B

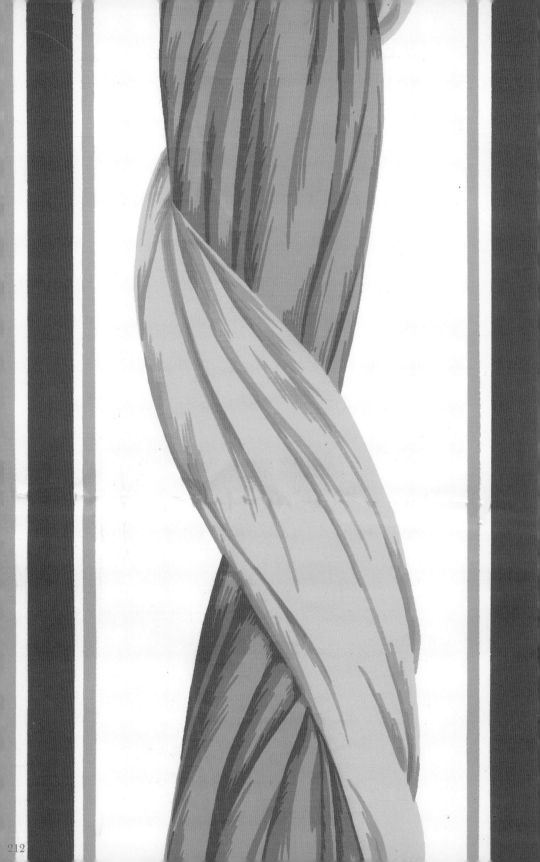

213A

213B

BLUE-VIOLET

evokes harmony.

Harmony in a room can be defined very much the same way as we think of harmony in music or poetry: a pleasing arrangement of different parts that appeals to the senses. When you're planning a blue-violet room, walk through a garden in full bloom and you'll most likely see many shades of blue-violet in the flower petals, beginning with a blush of reddish pink at the base and mixing with the brilliant blues.

When putting together a room featuring blue-violet, start with a soft shade of patterned pink on the ceiling and a shade of blue-violet on the wall to achieve the basis for a harmonious living space. Some of the most striking gardens are grown in predominantly one color; this approach to decorating a room can prove effective too.

Finally, when you are in the garden for inspiration, observe where the blue-violet resides in the shadows. It is an intriguing and harmonious color: two qualities that are at the core of every great room.

The walls—Andover Strie: Periwinkle (pages 226–227); the ceiling—Serenade Scroll: Periwinkle (page 231); the sofas—Neo-Classical Toile: Silver Blue and Sky (pages 220–221); the rug—Savona Swag Border: Blue on Sand (page 219); the screen—Lyla: Document Gold (page 83)

228A

228B

230B

231

VIOLET

is dignified.

Violet is a color that is as beautiful as its name. I think if musical instruments could express color, string instruments would emit violet in their sound. Violet has always been associated with royalty, full of pomp and history. In 331 B.C., Alexander the Great unearthed 190-year-old purple robes in the Royal Treasury in Susa (then the Persian capitol), believed to be worth millions. In the third century, a grave was discovered to contain the oldest dye recipe known to imitate purple, a color now known as Stockholm-Papyrus. At this time, silk garments dyed in purple were so expensive they were literally worth their weight in gold.

Violet is meditative and healing and supremely natural. I think of the smooth round stones with the purple cast you see along a beach or a rushing stream. The stones are worn, yet polished, and full of strength (red) and tranquility (blue). What a gorgeous room you can create using that combination.

Choose any shades of violet, mix with the soft gray tones of a misty morning sky, and accent with the complementary yellow of the afternoon sun. This combination will result in a statement of beauty and tranquility suitable for any room in your home.

The curtains, canopy and settee—Jodhpur Floral and Border: Mocha and Purple (page 236); the table skirt—Hadley Stripe: Purple and Green (pages 248–249); the carpet—Akita: Oatmeal (pages 278–279)

239A

239B

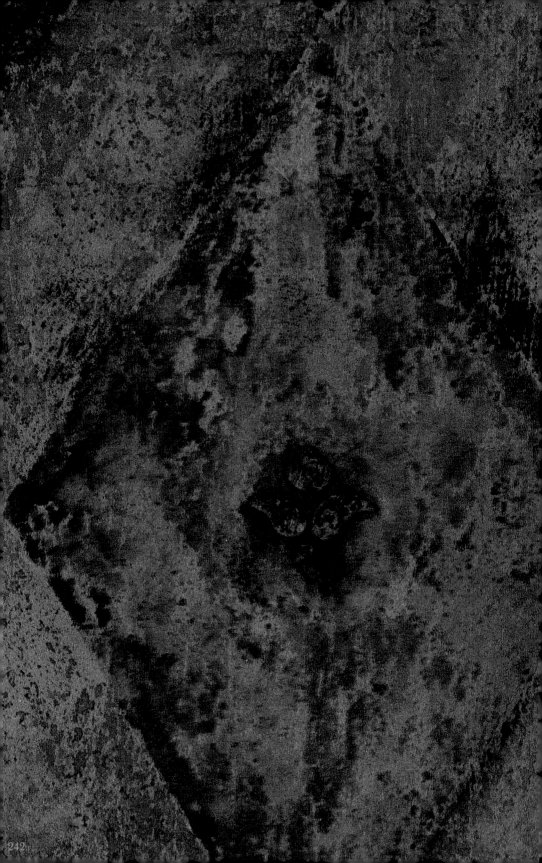

244A

244B   244 C

RED-VIOLET

evokes mystery.

Historically, the colors red and violet were reserved for royalty. Today, like an aged bottle of burgundy or the shiny skin of eggplants piled high at the farmers' market, red-violet is an extremely accessible, versatile, and rich color. Red-violet can be bright and punchy like magenta or soft and meditative like lilac.

Since red-violet is the color of a great red wine, it is particularly suited for a dining room. I find it very satisfying to spend time in a room full of shades and patterns of red-violet while enjoying the convivial atmosphere of a dinner with family and friends. Another way to bring red-violet indoors is through flowers, but instead of limiting yourself to the lifespan of a bouquet, why not live with beautiful florals on your walls all year long?

Keep in mind that shades of yellow-green are complementary to red-violet: creating a look with an acid green and magenta shades is very modern and can be quite liberating.

However you choose to decorate a room in red-violet—whether with a traditional claret damask or a contemporary lipstick hue—you will evoke an engaging richness suitable to any type of space.

The walls—Premier Strie: Scarlet (page 253); the wainscoting—Losange: Pewter (pages 276–277); the curtains—Feuillage Ombre: Red (page 262); the flooring—Fern Strie: Topaz (page 104)

253A

253B

255A

255B

256A

261A   261B

NEUTRAL

is natural.

Though I enjoy living with a lot of color, there is nothing quite like a room full of neutral tones. A neutral room is the perfect backdrop for showcasing a fine art or antiques collection, or a spectacular view.

One way to create a clean, contemporary look is with textured wallcoverings in the perennially fashionable beige and brown. It is easy to combine numerous bold patterns in the same room when the designs are based on the same natural hue.

Even though the majority of this book showcases an infinite variety of color and pattern, consider tempering the mood of a room with a balance of neutrals and color. Choose to simply cover one wall or the ceiling of a painted room to add an extra layer of interest, or paper a wooden valance with one or two of your favorite neutral designs as an accent to any room. Or cover the interior surfaces in your closets with a pattern, either in neutral or a color—it provides a pleasant surprise for whomever looks inside!

The walls—Botanical Scenic Toile: Onyx (pages 274–275); the wainscoting—Field Stripe: Beige (page 228); the tub—Petits Elephants: Ivory (page 284); the flooring—Country House: Ink (page 272); and last, but not least, the dog—Circus Toile: Black and White (pages 64–65)

278 B

288A

288B

INDEX

"Either that wallpaper goes, or I do."
>—Oscar Wilde, 1854–1900; his last words
before dying in a drab Paris hotel room

"He went; wallpaper is here to stay."
>—Author's Note

This index is designed to help you learn more about these available wallcoverings. The index listing is structured in the following fashion:

Title: Colorway (collection name), a brief description, and the page number where the pattern can be located.

Some terms used in the index may require defining:

Border: a width of wallpaper designed for use as trim on walls where they meet the ceiling; used as accents on a plain painted wall or with a coordinating wallcovering used throughout a room.

Colorway: the identifier for a pattern, chosen by the predominant color.

Damask: a design ornamented with flowered patterns or wavy lines.

Strie: a pattern with any number of parallel lines, stripes, or bands.

Moire: designs with a watered, or wavy, pattern.

Ombre: shaded or graduated in tone; said of a color.

Toile de Jouy: an eighteenth-century French scenic pattern usually printed in one color on a light ground.

Toss: seemingly random patterns, often on a solid background, that form a lightly and easily arrayed design.

A Note on the Collections

The historical and creative inspiration for some of the collections seen throughout the book are described below:

Asian Influence was inspired by the artwork of antique wallcoverings, embroidery, hand-painted silks, and stencilings that capture the singular beauty of the Far East.

Border Book V represents architectural patterns, as well as floral and ribbon, fruit and vegetable, contemporary, and children's designs. Borders came into prominence within Schumacher's high-end lines in the late 1970s, early 1980s, leading the trend toward the widespread availability and easy affordability of borders today.

Classic Essentials introduces an array of new stripes, combining them with Schumacher's most popular wallpapers and borders from previous collections. Innovative printing techniques add textural interest to these new stripes.

Classic Handprints (Volumes I—III) are companions of traditional Schumacher fabrics, reflecting neoclassical, oriental, and traditional influences.

Cuisine et Salle de Bains is richly laden with charming adapatations of fruits, vegetables, and sea life, creating a tranquil presence welcome in today's kitchen and baths.

Damask Edition highlights the versatility of this enduringly popular look, using medium- to large-scale designs, presented in a full palette, including luxurious metallics and soft hues, to impart elegance in any setting.

Designs for Men's strong designs feature stripes, paisleys, and plaids, as well as sporting and gaming themes, and is further distinguished by introducing several designs on such new tactile papers as cork, burlap, and flannel.

Dimensional Elements captures the subtle look of suede, the beguiling allure of snakeskin, the complexity of tortoiseshell, and the intricacy of frescoed walls in an exciting palette of such natural colors as jade, coral, alabaster, ivory, and cork.

Encore IV represents the most popular Schumacher papers from past collections, judged by their enduring popularity and timelessness of classic design. These range from background damasks to the more striking designs for which Schumacher is renowned.

En Vacances wallcoverings, with their country and coastal designs, are especially well-suited for vacation homes, consisting of patterns selected for their restful, restorative qualities.

Exotic Passage designs incorporate such natural elements as wicker and bamboo, and are energized with playful monkeys, colorful birds, and the meandering vines of tropical landscapes.

Garden Pleasures were created as companion pieces for a printed fabric line, with vines, blooming flowers, and stripes that transform any interior into a tranquil haven.

Garden Vines is primarily composed of popular flower and trellis patterns, offering sidewalls and borders that introduce the freshness of a garden into the home.

Grand Bazaar is rooted in the textile mastery of the ancient cultures encompassing the Near and Middle East, utilizing elements and designs found in such traditional Persian, Indian, Turkish, and Moorish furnishings as carpets, fabrics, and wall hangings.

Haberdashery's classically rendered designs feature paisleys and such strong geometrics as diamond-motifs and plaids, enlivened by a diversified palette of rich, saturated colors.

The Historic Natchez Collection captures the spirit and style of the rich decorative heritage of Natchez, the Mississippi River town famous for its great columned mansions and opulent interiors. The designs are derived from historic fabrics, papers, brassware, ceramics, furniture, and architecture.

India is based on artistic elements indigenous to the country, with exquisite designs found on turbans, saris, carpets, and in architecture.

Les Enfant's whimsical papers and borders for the young and young at heart feature cleverly inventive depictions of planes, harlequin jesters, animals, and butterflies playfully transformed into enchanting designs.

Make Believe offers clowns, boats, leaping frogs, fish, flowers, and musical monkeys to create lasting memories for a whole new generation.

Manor Classics was inspired by the luxurious fabrics of the Schumacher line; the designs range from charming floral and fruit botanicals reminiscent of the English countryside to the regal, neoclassical patterns found in sophisticated stately homes.

Mini Motifs are finely crafted and styled to create subtle, relaxing backgrounds perfectly suited for use alone or with larger floral patterns, geometrics, textures, or solids.

Natural Textures have been crafted from a variety of such materials as bamboo, grasses, paper weaves, cork, sisal, burlap, and arrowroot.

Neutral Collection represents Schumacher's most popular neutrals from various collections updated with additional neutral colorways and ranges from textures to full-scale damasks, toiles, stripes, and ombres.

Objets d'Arts will add a touch of drama in any room, comprised primarily of such fanciful novelty designs as butterflies, antique pocket watches, and handbags, and designed to build a foundation for a whimsical interior for those with an eye for collectibles.

Papiers de France offers the romantic artistry, delicacy, and charm that typify the French spirit, and is drawn from a rich heritage of designs from France.

Royal Retreats draws on the art, architecture, and furnishings of castles and estates in Britain, utilizing elements from tapestries, china, ironwork, paintings, and fine woodwork. Four prodigious estates—Blair Castle, Burghley House, Blenheim Palace, and Woburn Abbey—serve as the basis for the collection.

Royal Sweden reveals the influence of European design on the furnishings, artwork, and artifacts of Sweden's noble manors.

Small Offerings introduces a wide range of detailed small-scale designs with precisely crafted stripes, florals, scallops, and geometrics, featured on backgrounds such as stripes, pindots, and textures.

Stripes & Plaids, in a color palette ranging from muted to bold, offers versatile geometric designs compatible with an array of interiors including florals, textures, and wovens.

Surface Impressions, designed with subtle backgrounds in mind, combines simple, engaging motifs with dimensional effects ranging from layered textures to mottled antiquing.

Texture Collection highlights papers composed of fibers carefully woven into a wide variety of intriguing patterns available in colors ranging from pale neutrals to saturated tones.

Victorian Collection consists of designs inspired by documents found in the Schumacher archives, offering both historically accurate documentary colors as well as a palette consistent with today's decorating trends.

Viewpoints collection's subtle use of geometrics, stripes, and florals in clean, simple lines helps create texture and dimension with diffused and layered color, while metallic accents add reflective interest to these designs.

Williamsburg®: A Legacy of Style is based on documents in the Colonial Williamsburg archives that inspired these fresh interpretations of traditional designs, capturing elements from such diverse artifacts as textiles, quilts, ceramics, and tiles from as early as the seventeenth century. Many of the designs within this collection may have appeared on eighteenth-century wallpapers, but the poor survival rate of historic wallpapers has made the study of them more elusive than other aspects of interior decoration.

Please note that due to the number of wallcoverings found in this book, not all of the collections have been described above; the index may contain additional information for these collections.

Chanlong Stripe: Plum (White Jade) A fantasy landscape partnered with a floral pattern and laid on a dark ground with a stripe as bold in scale as it is subtle in tone. Pages 12–13 and 16–17 (Lacquer)

Florette Border: Rosewood (Petite Prints) An elegant trim, whether paired with a tonal wallcovering or a creamy yellow painted wall. Page 14

Islandia: Aubergine (The Archive Collection) A loosely rendered grass cloth in a deep wine color. Pages 14–15

Mandarin Dolls: Rosewood (White Jade) A looser feel on a traditional chinoisierie. Pages 15 and 33 (Aqua)

Chanlong Stripe: Lacquer (White Jade) Available in several colorways. Pages 12–13 (Plum) and 16–17

Grapevine Border: Garnet (Petite Prints) A naturally curving grapevine supported by the architecturally rigorous wrought-iron framework adds to the detail of this accent border. Page 17

Sutton Strie: Garnet (Petite Prints) A Chinese lacquer red strie. Page 18

Madison Damask: Red (Tones and Textures) Medium-scale tonal red-on-red damask. Page 18

Fern Strie: Garnet (Petite Prints) Geometric leaf pattern on a strie. Page 19

China Poem: Lacquer (White Jade) The tone-on-tone treatment of this Chinese writing creates a sophisticated colorway for an exotic wallcovering. Page 20

Canton Border: Fuchsia (White Jade) A beige Greek key supports the blossoming pattern. Page 21

Neo-Classical Toile: Cherry and Wood (Classic Handprints, Vol. II) Stunning, in several colorways. Pages 22–23 and 220–221 (Silver Blue and Sky)

Compass Point Border: Red (Haberdashery) A nautical accent for a study or a trophy room. Page 24

> "Scenic papers create tremendous depth in any room; when I use them, I feel as if I am creating a vista to another world."
>
> **—John Nalewaja, wallpaper restorer**

Hoffman Ring Border: Primary (Frank Lloyd Wright Collection) A geometric pattern in primary colors, suitably honoring the American master. Pages 24–25

Rosehill Damask: Brick (Summer Estate Archives) A tone-on-tone damask stimulates on a moire background. Pages 26–27

Bamboo Fret: Lacquer (White Jade) The delicacy of the geranium buds balanced with the strength of the bamboo latticework create an elegant wallcovering. Pages 27 and 29 (Parchment)

Linleigh Stripe: Berry (Summer Estate Archives) Inspired by the cotton ticking stripe. Pages 27–28

> "Wallpaper, *both* color and design, should be a background, not something out of *Little Shop of Horrors*. As Pauline Trigere said, 'When you feel blue, wear red.'"
>
> **—Stephen Stempler, Stephen Stempler Designs, Inc.**

Windsor Scroll Border: Peacock (The Archive Collection) A royal border to finish a painted wall or to be properly paired with a complementary papered wall. Page 28

Bamboo Fret: Parchment (White Jade) A scented geranium peeks through an elegant bamboo fret. Available in several colorways. Pages 27 (Lacquer) and 29

Rockwood Floral: Document (The Archive Collection) Large-scale tropical parrots and parrot tulips to enliven any size garden room. Page 30

Haverhill: Primary (Portraits of America) An arabesque play, birds on swings with scenic landscapes in a diamond-shape lozenge. Page 31

Pompom Arabesque Border: Cameo (Petite Prints) Pink pompoms play in this serpentine border. Page 32

Althorp Floral: Coral (Arboretum) Roses prettier than Redoute grace this floral design. Pages 32–33

> "Color and pattern are the life and soul of a room; without them the room can't help but have the blahs. The fastest way to add pizzazz to a room is to hang it with a smart wallpaper."
>
> **—Michael D. Devine, Senior fashion editor, *HFN Magazine***

Mandarin Dolls: Aqua (White Jade) A looser feel on a traditional chinoiserie. Pages 15 (Rosewood) and 33

Portraits of America: Cottage Red (Portraits of America) For an instant historical feel to any entranceway or living room, this damask is the answer. Page 26

Rosebud Vine: Parchment (Petite Prints) A climbing-rose pattern on a moire background. Page 27

Millington: Brick (Portraits of America) An American flower stencil, stylized ribbon. Page 27

Brimfield Floral: Red (Portraits of America) This toss, set against a spidery vine background, is aged by the mutedness of the colorway. Page 36

"You should never notice the color in a room; rather, you should notice the mood and ambiance the room creates with its color—warm, cool, dramatic, cozy—whether it's the simplest beige sponging or the most intense cinnabar lacquer."
—Renny Reynolds, designer

Rosette and Ribbon Border: Cameo (Petite Prints) A perfect marriage of a soft colorway and an even softer architectural sculpting makes this accent appropriate for the bedroom or bath. Page 37

Strathmore Texture: Cameo (Petite Prints) The subtlety of this print can support a bold pattern used elsewhere in the same room. Pages 37 and 108 (Topaz)

La Pagode Border: Jade (White Jade) Finely detailed images of Cathay dance across this charming chinoiseire border. Page 38

Parakeets: Wedgwood (Portraits of America) Parrots on parade on a muted colonial colorway. Pages 38–39

White Point Garden: Cream (The Archive Collection) Transitional whimsical floral vine. Page 39

"Pink is the navy blue of India."
—Diana Vreeland

Pallav Elephants: Cream and Pink (India) A reverential treatment to all things India: the incredible hues, the fine embroidery, and the regal elephant. Page 40

Windsor Diamond: Rose (The Archive Collection) A tufted trompe l'oeil of royal pedigree. Page 42

Primavera Floral: Blush (Arboretum) The first blush of spring on pinstripes. Page 42

Colonial Toile: Document Red (Portraits of America) A play on scale where the posies are prepesterously larger than the people. Page 43

Poor Richard's Toile: Coral (Portraits of America) "A small leak will sink a great ship" and plenty of other sayings in cameo settings. Pages 44–45

Greenhouse Wall: Terra-cotta (Trompe L'Oeil) The solidity of marble without the expense. Pages 44–45

Canton Vine: Natural (White Jade) Wild roses discovered by nineteenth-century plantsmen in China and transplanted onto this gorgeous wallcovering. Page 46

Summer Lea: Blush (Arboretum) A subtle meadow laden with ornamental grasses, snails, and butterflies. Page 47

Diamond Basketweave: Petal (Arboretum) The title says it all. A stunning print. Page 48

Hewitt Scallop: Rose (Portraits of America) An abstract repeat of stylized scallops. Page 49

Federal Basket: Petal (Portraits of America) Stenciled beige blossoms on a petal strie from early nineteenth-century American basket. Page 49

"All colors go together—it is really all about combinations and perspective. People will make limiting statements, like, 'I hate maroon'—but I'll counter with 'Have you ever seen Nureyev's living room in Paris?' Embossed leather, in maroon, with flecks of gilt! Fabulous." —Miles Redd, designer

Modena: Red (Surface Impressions) Stylized arabesques in a painterly fashion to resemble a fresco. Page 52

Izmir Stripe: Terra-cotta and Sage (Grand Bazaar) A striped East Indian pattern resembling an Ikat textile. Page 52

Oushak: Lacquer (Grand Bazaar) Based on an Indian rug. Page 53

"I always encourage my clients to use color and pattern. Yet one would think the entire world was Navajo white. Try it! You might like it! Set yourself and your space apart." —Roderick N. Shade, Roderick N. Shade, Inc.

Cordelia: Coral (Portraits of America). Eighteenth-century floral intertwined with a diamond trellis design. Pages 53–54

Petits Palmiers: Lacquer (Exotic Passage) A plethora of palm trees sure to raise the temperature of any room. Page 54

Panama Wicker Border: Red (Exotic Passage) Trompe l'oeil wicker-weave border to punctuate a neutral or red lacquer surface. Page 55

Flaxen Stripe: Red (Dimensional Elements) Textural stripe that simulates a faux design. Page 55

"Use wallpaper on the ceiling to create a visual pattern to lead one's eye up."
—Eve Robinson, Eve Robinson Associates, Inc.

Mako Texture: Red (Dimensional Elements) With this faux sharkskin, there is safety in numbers; paper numerous walls in a game room, finished den, or study. Pages 56–57

Karachi: Peach and Aqua (Grand Bazaar) Transport any room in your home to the Far East with this exotic print. Pages 56–57

Fossilized Leaf: Cinnabar (Dimensional Elements) Both the seemingly handcrafted nature of this print and welcoming colorway add to its timelessness. Page 57

Lucente: Terra-cotta (Dimensional Elements) A meticulous shimmering copper field. Page 58

Honeycomb Texture: Carnelian (Dimensional Elements) As bees are drawn to honey, designers are drawn to this abstract design again and again. Page 58

Airlie Bouquet: Cream and Aqua (Historic Natchez Collection, Volume III) This arabesque design is an adaptation of an early twentieth-century printed cotton document found in a dependency building at Airlie, a late eighteenth-century rambling cottage on the outskirts of Natchez. Page 59

Alcott Plaid: Coral (Stripes & Plaids) A wallpaper you could wear. Available in several colorways. Pages 60–61 and 193 (Green)

Prescott Stripe: Cream and Coral (Stripes & Plaids) A handsome stripe with a carnelian pinstripe accent. Page 60

Hadley Stripe: Coral and Green (Stripes & Plaids) Stripes with an interplay of color to cheer up any room. In a variety of colorways. Page 61

"Powder and dining rooms are by their nature rooms to have fun with. Go the extra distance and inject fantasy through the use of wallpaper."
—Matthew Patrick Smyth, designer

Indienne Vine: Jute (Williamsburg: Pure, Simple, Today, Vol. I) A charming Indienne on a woven textural background. Page 62

Mary Rose Toss: Sage Green (Williamsburg: Pure, Simple, Today, Vol. I) The random beauty of roses. Page 62

Silk Flower Sidewall: Red (Vintage Textiles) A dreamy transparency: the spontaneity of watercolor secured in the permanence of a wallcovering. Page 63

Circus Toile: Raspberry (Make Believe, Les Enfants) A fun take on toile: children will want to run away with this circus. Pages 64–65

> **"I always say, 'Orange is the navy blue of Mexico.'"**
> **—T. Keller Donovan, designer**

La Frutta: Antique Gold (Bella Tuscany) This juicy pattern will add immediate flavor to a redesigned kitchen. Pages 68–69

Vernon Multi Stripe: Purple and Green (Textural Classics) The volume and local color of this border are what make this design a textural classic. Page 69

Barbados Cane: Red (Small Offerings) Delicate latticework in a very bold color-way makes a handsome backdrop for a study or unconventional office. Pages 70 and 124 (Yellow)

Holly Filligree: Red (Small Offerings) Pair this with a midnight-blue paper and watch the colors vibrate: a great solution for enlivening any space. Pages 70–71

Tuscan Fruit Border: Red (Via Siena) With minimal expense, edge your kitchen ceilings with this fruit border and transform your space instantly. Pages 71–73

Exotic Palm Texture: Coral (New York Botanical Gardens: A Visit to the Garden) This tone-on-tone treatment makes a fairly dense pattern much more accessible for use in the home. Page 72

Tuscan Urn Border: Clay (Via Siena) A terrific complement to any terra-cotta stonework incorporated into your home design. Page 73

Chelsea Botanical Lattice: Antique (Wlliamsburg: A Legacy of Style) This large-scale pattern is useful for opening up the space of a small room. Pages 74–75 and 162 (Cream and Aqua)

Tidewater Resist: Colonial Red (Williamsburg: Pure, Simple, Today) The batik effect used on this landscape serves as a direct link back to the candlemakers of Williamsburg. Page 74

Indienne Border: Sage Green (Williamsburg: Pure, Simple, Today) The warm tones of this border will envelop a room nicely; use it against a cream wall or a solid-papered wall. Pages 76–77

Mary Rose Stripe: Peach (Williamsburg: Pure, Simple, Today) Sweet and simple: paper your cupboards or tabletops with this inviting stripe. Pages 76–77

> **"Stripes are the great equalizer. They make the subtle, bold; the short, tall; the wide, slim; the average, regal; the grand, approachable. Stripes, indeed, give one a great feeling of hope."**
> **—Ron Alose, Ron Alose Design Group Ltd.**

Linares Strie: Coral and Green (Stripes & Plaids) The unique approach of applying this palette to a stripe pays high dividends: imagine the joy of cooking in a kitchen surrounded with such a fresh color treatment. Pages 76–77

Indienne Stripe: Sage Green (Williamsburg: Pure, Simple, Today) The textured printing on this paper sets it apart from a standard stripe; a great companion with the Indienne Border (above). Page 77

Document Prints: Tea Stain (New York Botanical Gardens: A Visit to the Garden) The exquisite shading on this paper adds to its delicacy, and the broad spacing of the botanicals speaks to the decisiveness of the overall affect. Page 78

Document Orchard: Beige (New York Botanical Gardens: A Visit to the Garden) Fairly muted colorway; totally fresh renderings to complete a kitchen or pantry. Page 79

Gardener's Toss: Primary (New York Botanical Gardens: A Visit to the Garden) A kitchen or workroom will be infinitely more cheerful once papered in this spritely pattern. Page 79

Britton's Rocaille: Red on Yellow (Victorian Collection) Small-scale Victorian cartouche with a delicate rosebud focus. Page 82

Ruth Audley Rose: Fuchsia and Yellow (Historic Natchez, Vol. III) Lush and lavish addition to any color-impoverished decor. Page 83

Lyla: Document Gold (Williamsburg: A Legacy of Style) These trailing lines can be seen on a bed quilt in the Colonial Williamsburg collection. The antique was made in England from 1700–1725 and is considered a masterpiece of design and execution. Available in several colorways. Pages 83 and 185 (Aqua)

Shield's Town House Vine: Yellow (Historic Natchez, Vol. III) The wildness of nature is tamed in this print suitable for kitchens and dining rooms. Page 84

Monkey Music Border: Yellow (Make Believe) Surprise a child by trimming his or her room with this border and strike up the band! Page 86

Stars N' Stripes: Yellow (Make Believe) Gorgeous tone-on-tone treatment makes for a stellar constellation. Pages 85–86

Botanical Chintz: Primrose (Williamsburg: A Legacy of Style) A direct descendant from the wallpapers of yesteryear, beautifully printed on a sturdy ground. Page 87

Lanai Floral: Yellow (Classic Handprints, Vol. III) A bold, large-scale print for the daring. Page 88

Cherry Grove Bough: Butter Yellow (Historic Natchez, Vol. III) Let every day be springtime with this stunning print. Page 89

Jungle Parade Border: Yellow (Make Believe) The minimal expense of a border is disproportionate to the design impact and ability to transform a child's room with ease. Page 90

Jake's Jester: Yellow (Les Enfants) This wallpaper presents a challenge for those children who want to wake up in a grumpy mood. Page 91

Abington Leaf: Yellow (Damask III) Tone-on-tone and placed on a moire background: transform a living room or parlor into an extraordinary gathering place. Page 92

Logan's Landing: Yellow (Les Enfants) Antique biplanes crisscross a sunshine-yellow sky, enabling youngsters to fly to dreamland with the help of this aviation print. Page 93

Chinese Flowers: Yellow (Williamsburg: A Legacy of Style) This swirl of activity will energize any space; use with discretion. Page 94

Confetti Pary: Yellow (Make Believe) A toss of a toss! Celebrate both color *and* pattern with this joyous design. Page 95

Zevatta Border: Buttercup (Make Believe) The energy never flags in this circus romp when used as a trim around the ceiling of a children's room. Pages 94–95

"Wallcoverings are a chameleon. They can enhance the proportion of a room or hide its imperfections."
—Todd Gribben, designer at Bunny Williams, Inc.

Feuillage Ombre: Yellow (Damask, Edition III) A mesmerizing print with a variety of color options. Page 96

Chinese Pavilion: Yellow (Garden Pleasures) A Chuck Fischer original. Acrobatic monkeys on a palm tree against a harlequin background. Page 97

Siaconsett Trellis: Yellow (Classic Handprints, Vol. III) Evocative of a morning in Nantucket. Page 98

Lots of Dots: Yellow (Les Enfants) The sunny disposition of this wallcovering is contagious. Page 98

Edwardian Imberline: Yellow (Damask, Edition III) Damask on an imberline, two different constructions, achieved through a visual woven process. Page 99

"Soup beginning a good meal is like a room with a great beginning, i.e., an interesting background—be it stripes, checks, a small print or a large one or a draped fabric design, always finished with a border or ribbon outlining the good architecture of a room. Sort of like the inside of a Victorian box of chocolates!" **—Mario Buatta, a.k.a. the Prince of Chintz**

Monkey Marching Band: Yellow (Make Believe) Impossible to resist. Pages 100–101

Fern Strie: Topaz (Petite Prints) The richness of the color supporting the precious ferns is what distinguishes this print. Page 104

Toile Arabesque: Yellow and Red (Historic Savannah II) Southerners have a way of telling a story, even with wallcoverings as the medium. A wildly sophisticated print, with a confident cross-hatching, and linear treatment. Page 105

Swedish Fish: Sunshine (Make Believe) Perfectly uniform, perfectly Swedish, perfectly enchanting. An engaging wallcovering for a child's room. Page 106

Clarendon Hills Texture: Gold (Country Manor) This wallcovering serves as a tour guide to a fantastical English countryside. Pages 107–108

Arbor Botanical Border: Sunflower (Woods and Meadows) A passing parade of twigs and blossoms suspended in the air over a two-toned sunflower ground and sandwiched between a bold red stripe. Pages 106–107

Strathmore Texture: Topaz (Petite Prints) The fine grain of a stationery bond is replicated here in this unexpectedly pleasing print. Pages 37 (Cameo) and 108

Neoclassical Stripe: Spice (Summer Estate Archives) Tradition rules in this classic print. Page 109

Greenbrier Vine: Sunflower (Woods and Meadows) The surprising shadowing on this design artfully emphasizes the fresh treatment of this fairly standard nature scene. Page 110

Bramble and Fern: Sunflower (Woods and Meadows) An inviting thicket of color and pattern; a terrific transitional paper for a sunroom or porch to bridge the outdoors with your inner sanctum. Page 110

Le Toile du Marche: Gold (Blue Ribbon, Showcase Collection) The historic region of central France inspired the two-dimensional rendering in this country print. Page 111

Greenwich Check: Buttercream (Portraits of America) Look closely and note the bird's eggs nestled in a cushiony home; the miniature floral print within the framework evokes a picnic table's oilcloth covering. Page 112

Telfair Star: Gold (Historic Savannah II) Our ancestral designers could have let this historic pattern become overwhelming, but they wisely negated that possibility with the tone-on-tone treatment in this rich, gold colorway. Page 112

Lynwood Strie: Sunflower (Woods and Meadows) The evocative wood grain is used to emphasize nature's ready-made design tools: texture and pattern. Page 113

Linleigh Stripe: Sunflower (Woods and Meadows) Hung vertically, the stripe mimics sunlight hitting a forest floor; placed horizontally, it is daylight muted by the barrier of a venetian blind. Page 113

Laurel Vine Border: Buttercream (Classic Handprints, Vol. II) Entwined leafs and berries in a beaded border. Page 114

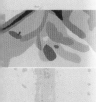

Greenbrier Border: Sunflower (Woods and Meadows) Twig cartouche surrounds a botanical portrait with butterflies. Pages 114–115

Twig and Berry Border: Sunflower (Woods and Meadows) And ladybugs, too! Bring the outdoors inside with this refreshing accent to a painted or papered wall. Page 115

Taylor's Stripe: Yellow (Les Enfants) This engaging use of a bold stripe will enliven any child's room instantly. Page 116

Taylor's Toss: Yellow (Les Enfants) With its charming imagery, this is one of the best-selling patterns in the collection. Pages 116–117

Haverhill: Yellow (Portraits of America) The trompe l'oeil effect displayed here—combining an aviary with art history artifacts—is heightened by the crackled ground that simulates a weather-worn stone wall. Page 118

Hancock Basket: Yellow (Portraits of America) The metallic gold adds luster to this large-scale print, lightening a room with ease. Page 118

Betsy's Garden: Cornsilk (Portraits of America) The naivete of this painting alludes to a simpler time. Page 119

Twinkle Twinkle: Aqua and Yellow (Make Believe) Star light, star bright, wallpaper your ceiling tonight. Page 119

Clarendon Hills Border: Gold (Country Manor) A stately and historical border of English heritage. Page 120

Tisbury Scallop: Blue and Yellow (Small Offerings) This repetitive, small-scale scalloped design defines charm. Page 120

Trevor's Tents: Yellow and Blue (Les Enfants) Trompe l'oeil painting of a canvas tent. Page 121

Davenport Scroll: Yellow (Historic Savannah II) The screen door background here gives the vine enough space to attach to as it ventures upward. Page 122

Mayfair Stripe: Sunflower (Woods and Meadows) The scalloped, ribbonlike trim serves to distinguish this design from that of a less stylish stripe. Page 123

Brimfield Vine: Buttercream (Portraits of America) The subtle vinework seen in close-up becomes an abstract crackled treatment when viewed from a distance. Page 123

Rose Hill: Buttercup (Summer Estate Archives). The gardener worked overtime on this lush print; a large-scale floral design ripe for the picking. Page 124

Barbados Cane: Yellow (Small Offerings) The British imported this design from the countryside on the easternmost island of the West Indies. Pages 70 (Red) and 124

Millington: Cornsilk (Portraits of America) The diamond-shaped pattern surrounds the floral portraits in this classic print. Page 125

Branford Damask: Yellow (Portraits of America) Inspired by handicrafts of our forebears, this timeless print softens and soothes. Page 125

Taki Bamboo: Yellow (Small Offerings) This airy pattern has the power to make a small room seem larger. Page 126

Fontaine Bleu: Yellow (Blue Ribbon) A Chuck Fischer original. Infuses the neoclassic elements of ornament with the winds of whimsy. A contemporary design available in three colorways. Page 127

> **"Scenic wallpaper can magically give a windowless box—a room—a splendid view or bring a faux garden indoors."**
> **—Todd Klein, designer**

Palm Trellis: Camel (Blue Ribbon) A Chuck Fischer original. A painterly rendering of exotic palm leaves, available in four colorways. Pages 130 and 139 (in Cream)

A Visit to the Garden: Natural (New York Botanical Garden) Ready-made frames surround these elegant renderings. Page 131

Empire Lampas: Green (Manor Classics) This foil damask supported by a tone-on-tone stripe greets visitors in the lobby of the design headquarters of the F. Schumacher & Co. Page 132.

Dorset Molding: Green (Classic Handprints, Vol. III). A trompe l'oeil treatment of the pressed tin ceilings of yesteryear add architectural gravitas to any ceiling. Pages 132–133

La Grande Border: Sand (Hallways) The sweep of this design belies the comparatively small surface coverage of a border. Page 134

Fresco Stripe: Green (Vintage Textiles) The tightness of the cheesecloth weave on this ground serves as ample support for the weight and boldness of the overall pattern. Page 135

Leopard Skin: Stone (Two by Two) A medium-scale tone-on-tone leopard print, its boldness slightly subdued by the muted colorway. Page 135

Bedford: Sage (Hallways) The contemporary play with the reverse silhouettes enlivens this traditional print. Page 136

Windorah Willow: Sage (Pergola) It's a lot to ask of a wallpaper: to be beautiful, affordable, and timeless. This one achieves all three. Page 136

> **"Well-drawn wallpaper never goes out of style."**
> **—Jason Kontos, editor, *Victoria* magazine**

Springport Trellis: Olive Green (Pergola) Butterflies are free in this briar patch; an irresistible addition to a garden room or playroom. Page 137

Sichuan: Sun Yellow (Pergola) A large-scale print, alluding to history both via the muted colorway and the weight of the subject matter. Page 138

Lawrence Stripe: Spring Green (Pergola) The vibration between the negative and positive space make this a lively stripe for a kitchen or sewing room. Page 139

"Walls give you the ability to take the viewer wherever you want to take them. They set the stage!"

—**Marc Corbin, designer**

Windowsill Orchid: Tea Tree (Blue Ribbon) The distinctive form of this perennial make this design a perennial favorite in the Schumacher collection. Page 140

Tropical Rain: Green on Pale Yellow (Blue Ribbon) A Chuck Fischer original. This leafy interlacing of palm fronds captures the dreamy steaminess of the oasis. The endpapers of this book show the same design in a different colorway. Pages 141 and pages 282–283 (in Wheat on Wheat)

Johanna: Celery (Blue Ribbon) This generously scaled pattern features the bounties of a particularly lush harvest season. An homage to the copious delights of summer. Page 142

Julia: Spring Green (Blue Ribbon) There may be nothing sweeter than a fine print on a *matelasse*. Garlands of flowers lined up in precise furrowlike stripes, with the more voluptuous blooms occupying wider stripes and the more delicate blossoms held in quiet containment. Page 143

Julia Vine: Spring Green (Blue Ribbon) A perfect complement to Julia, either in an entranceway or on an adjoining wall. Page 143

Pergola: Sage (Pergola) This chinoserie print can quickly add an authoritative historical flair to any room. Pages 144–145

Marion Toss: Limestone (Hallways) The delicacy of these exquisitely rendered botanicals contrasts beautifully with the solidity of the faux limestone background. Page 145

Samantha: Multi on Mint (Small Offerings) Seek out the tiny bouquets in this soft, fresh ground of mint. Page 146

Frog Serenade: Light Green (Make Believe) This fantasy mural will delight children (and children-at-heart) with its whimsy and joy. Pages 146–147

"A doctor can bury his mistakes, but an architect can only advise his client to plant vines."

—**Frank Lloyd Wright**

Fox Hound Border: Charcoal (Tone on Tone II) The finishing touch for a hunting lodge loaded with dark wood and overstuffed furniture. Pages 150–151

Ningbo Sisal: Hunter (Texture Collection) Inspired by the weavers of the Zhejiang province in East China. Page 150

Lacquered Strie: Green (Classic Handprints, Vol. III) This paper's sheen adds to the sophistication of the tonal treatment. Page 151

Burghley Grill: Forest (Royal Retreats) A salute to William Cecil Burghley, the English statesman and advisor to Elizabeth I. Page 151

Fox Hound Border: Green (Tone on Tone II) For canine lovers who don't hesitate to announce that fact. Page 152

Leaf Parquet: Dark Green (Mini Motifs) Pressed leaves on a latticework ground harken back to the youthful joy of handmade craft projects. Page 153

Andrea Gimp Border: Green and Ivory (Mini Motifs) This border implies a ribbon-like braided fabric sometimes stiffened with wire and used to trim garments and furniture. Page 154

Tiffany Rose: Ivory on Dark Green (Mini Motifs) These buds hint at growing possibility, adding to the paper's currency and design relevancy. Page 154

Dianthus: Green (Mini Motifs) The medium scale on this toss of carnations adds to its exuberant feel. Page 155

"When I finally get to install the wallcoverings that were usually chosen or designed and handmade many months before, there is an immediate transformation of a room from an empty space to a space pulled together and complete." —Nancy Boszhardt, designer at Bunny Williams, Inc.

Blair Castle Damask: Green (Royal Retreats) Both a historical homage and an au courant design choice. Page 156

Blenheim Damask: Green (Royal Retreats) Add immediate royal heft to any interior design with this paper inspired by documents at this fabulous English country house. Page 157

Eternal Flame Border: Empire Green (Manor Classics) This pattern's solemnity is offset by the lushness of the color treatment. Page 158

Highland Argyle: Green (Royal Retreats) This harlequin argyle is bold in the unique simplicity of its design. Page 159

Laurel Leaf Border: Green and Yellow (Garden Vines) A fresh accent. Pages 158–159

Basketweave Strie: Green (Tone on Tone II) Texture and tone in a tight weave; available in several colorways. Pages 160 and 164 (Leaf)

Strawberry Ombre: Berry and Green (Mini Motifs) Strawberry fields forever: this sophisticated, country-flavored dense pattern is perfect for any kitchen or pantry. Pages 160–161

Morganti Stripe: Green (Manor Classics) A stately design choice when leaning toward a striped wallcovering. Page 161

Chelsea Botanical Lattice: Cream and Aqua (Williamsburg: A Legacy of Style) The coolness of this colorway adds significantly to the air and lightness of this large-scale design. Pages 74–75 (Antique) and 162

Fern Ombre: Teal (Tone on Tone II) Bring the softness and intrigue of a forest floor onto your walls with this simple design. Page 163

Basketweave Strie: Leaf (Tone on Tone II) Texture and tone in a tight weave; available in several colorways. Pages 160 (Green) and 164

Les Poulets: Sand (Classic Handprints, Vol. III) Enliven a kitchen or country dining room with this charming barnyard landscape. Pages 164–165

Antibes Stripe: Green (En Vacances) A soothing stripe for a calming effect in any home decor. Page 166

"If color is mood, pattern is personality—some have it, some don't"
—Deborah Sanders, editor, *Veranda* magazine

Spring Woods: Celadon (Garden Vines) A room laden with windows overlooking a garden or wooded lot and papered in this pattern will give the illusion of bringing the outdoors inside. Available in several colorways. Pages 166–167 (Celadon) and 173 (Green on White)

Mottled Stripe: Forest (Tone on Tone II) This stripe is a natural offshoot of the desire to bring natural motifs indoors. Page 167

Narcissus Trellis: Green (Manor Classics) You'll love yourself for choosing this beautiful floral repeat, available in several colorways. Pages 168–169

Ornamental Garden: Soft Green (En Vacances) Snapshot portraits of outdoor discoveries are endlessly enchanting in this bold repeat. Pages 169 (Soft Green) and 172 (Leaf and Cream)

Catania Toile: Green and Cream (Garden Pleasures) This large-scale floral pattern was inspired by the lush greenery found in and around the seaport on the east coast of Sicily. Pages 170–171

"For the under-forty crowd, wallpaper is but a magazine. After reading this info-packed tome, we can look forward to a new generation of crazed wall-covering aficionados."
—John Danzer, Munder-Skiles

Flower Lattice: Green (Mini Motifs) The small scale of this dense pattern forms a calming repeat when used on a broad expanse of wall. Page 174

Lucien Border: Green (Garden Pleasures) Ancient Greek scrolls are evoked in this sturdy, linked design. Page 174

Chairs of the Continent: Green and White (Objets D'Arts) Using the simple elegance of these line drawings to communicate the boldness of each chair's personality creates a uniquely balanced backdrop for any sitting room or parlor. Page 175

Tropique Border: Orange and Chocolate (Classic Handprints, Vol. II) The boldness and brightness of a Caribbean vacation, muted here with the black-as-ink ground. Pages 178–179

Elghammar Medallion: Blue (Royal Sweden) An existing wallpaper at Elghammar manor is the inspiration for this pattern. The regal arrangement of scattered medallions on a solid ground is indicative of the clean continental motifs found in Swedish design. Page 180

Jaipur Turban Stripe: Blue and Green (India) Inspired by the bold textiles of the Far East. Pages 180–181

Cori Circle: Teal (Damask II) The complexity of this intricate interlocking pattern mesmerizes; use with discretion. Pages 180–181

Baku Texture: Teal (Grand Bazaar) Inspired by a woven textile and updated with a modern color. Page 182

La Carte: Blue (Objets d'Arts) Suitable for the dreamer's room in any house: a meditation room, library, or bedroom. Page 183

Ovedskloster Stripe: Silver and Jade (Royal Sweden) The invention of the tiled stove in 1767 had a major effect on Swedish interiors: not only heat-efficient, they were also beautifully decorated. This design, taken from an existing faience stove at Ovedskloster, gives the look of a hand-drawn stripe with a cracked finish. Page 184

Harlowe Damask: Blue (Damask III) This reverse-silhouette floral pattern hints at hidden depths and intrigue; the mystery of what to do with that one troubling room is solved. Page 184

Lyla: Aqua (Williamsburg: A Legacy of Style) These trailing lines can be seen on a bed quilt in the Colonial Williamsburg collection. The antique was made in England between 1700–1725 and is considered to be a masterpiece of design and execution. Pages 83 (Document Gold) and 185

"As designers we are so jaded with the surfeit of available design . . . that it takes the 'dynamic' to make us sit up and notice. For sheer brilliance, no one did it better than the late Keith Haring. The unforgettable imagery of the *Vanity Fair* shoot by Annie Liebowitz featured a buck-naked Haring, his body self-painted in signature black and white graffiti, juxtaposed against a wall of the same design. . . . Totally surreal and a truly definitive 'wallcovering moment.'"

—**Geoffrey N. Bradfield, designer**

Rosa di Sardinia: Document Aqua (Classic Handprints, Vol. II) Stately bouquets in urns in exquisite juxtaposition to the delicate trompe l'oeil of the floral lacework. Page 186

Kashi Khan: Aqua Multi (Asian Influence) This large-scale floral pattern actually has a raised feel to it, immeasurably adding to its liveliness. Page 187

Strie Stripe: Cerulean (Tone on Tone II) A perfect complement to a bold pattern when placed on a facing or adjacent wall. Page 188

Sea Island Stripe: Green (Cuisine et Salle de Bains) Freshness personified. Pages 188 and 209 (Aqua)

Gracie Stripe: Cyprus (Classic Essentials) Total tone is often the essential background component for showcasing art or framed photographs to their best advantage. Pages 189 and 229 (Sky); see book's cover (Raspberry).

Ahmedabad Stripe: Aqua (India) Inspired by the airiest of textiles: a breath of fresh air in a kitchen or sitting room. Pages 189 and 244–245 (Purple)

La Frise Rustique Border: Document Robin's Egg (Garden Pleasures) This leafy, rustic border in nature's calming blue-green tones, adds a soothing touch to a country kitchen or breakfast nook. Page 190

Palm Trellis: Cream (Garden Pleasures) A Chuck Fischer original. Opt to paper a room in this pattern and have a vacation getaway within walking distance at all times. Page 191

Serenissima: Blue (Damask Edition) Not many large-scale patterns can so easily inspire the joyousness of this floral design. Page 192

Alcott Plaid: Green (Stripes & Plaids) Simplicity redefined; available in several subtle colorways. Pages 60–61 (Coral) and 193

Shantou Shade: Blue (Asian Influence) This exquisite replica of an Asian paper shade equates instant sophistication in an entranceway or bedroom. Page 194

Fish Mosaic: Pale Blue (Cuisine et Salle de Bains) Price out a tiled bathroom, then rejoice in the affordability of this cool, fresh replica. Available in several colorways. Page 195

Marcella Damask: Jade (Damask III) This medium-scale design makes good use of the principle of directional arrows, which constantly lead the eye around a room, and makes this a keenly fresh wallpaper. Page 196

Rosaria Damask: French Blue (Damask Edition) The dark shadows serve to make the lighter floral pattern seemingly pop off the wall, without the expense of a flocked paper. Page 196

Andover Strie: Turquoise (Classic Essentials) A stalwart of the Schumacher collection, available in a variety of colorways, to meet any decorating needs. Page 197

Lido Damask: French Blue (Damask Edition) A hint of color, a hint of pattern: the height of good taste. Page 197

> "All colors are friends of their neighbors and the lovers of their opposites."
> —W.H. Auden

Royal Crowns: Royal Blue & Gold (Royal Sweden) A wallpaper fit for a king. Page 200

Aurora Borealis: Lapis (Viewpoint) Celestial stargazing at its finest; dare to wallpaper a ceiling. Pages 199–200

Franklin Foulard: Blue (Haberdashery) Reminiscent of the classic men's cravat. Pages 202–203

Bermuda Race: Midnight (Haberdashery) Nautical poetry in motion. Page 203

Star of India: Indigo (India) A jewel in the crown of any interior. Page 204

Palmettes de Cachemire Border: Navy (Papiers de France) Paisley perfection in a border redux. Page 204

Palmettes de Cachemire: Navy (Papiers de France) Paisley perfection on a grand scale. Page 205

Toile Fleurie: Indigo (Papiers de France) The simplicity of this colorway—almost, but not quite, black and white—serves to balance the cacophony of this incredible foliage pattern. Pages 206–207

Stencil Leaf: Blue (Viewpoint) A subtle sponge print in the softest of blues, sure to relax anyone reclining nearby in the boudoir. Page 208

Lilu : Royal Blue (Encore IV) Originally from an Asian collection, this detail from a textile creates a beautiful dense overall design. Page 208

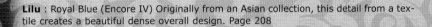

Sea Island Stripe: Aqua (Cuisine et Salles de Bains) Stripe it rich with this bold pattern. Pages 188 (Green) and 209

Ornamental Volute Border: Blue on White (Encore IV) Classic rope border to frame any room. Page 210

L'Indienne: Blue on White (Papiers de France) Classic French indienne design gives a little kiss to any wall. Page 211

Drape Twist Border: Yellow and Blue (Encore IV) Such a clever trompe l'oeil as this is often the perfect finishing touch in a room. Page 212

Feuilles Baies: Blue and Yellow on White (Papiers de France) Pineapple and berries to enliven any kitchen. Page 213

Gujarat Stencil: Yellow and Blue (India) A valentine to Paul Scott, the author of *Jewel in the Crown*. Page 213

Leaves of Blair Athol: Blue (Royal Retreats) Bring *House of Blue Leaves*–inspired designs into the home. Page 214

Kittery: Blue (Cuisines et Salle de Bains) Creamware stencil on a beautiful Wedgwood blue background. Page 214

Cordova Fruited Vine: Blue (Cuisine et Salle de Bains) Dragonflies airily averting the winding grapevine will add precious breathing space to any garden room or bath incorporating this pattern. Page 215

"There is no such thing as a bad color—just bad use of color."
—**Thad Hayes, designer**

Virginia Lee: Cobalt (Historic Natchez, Vol. III) A leafy scroll pattern. Page 218

Savona Swag Border: Blue on Sand (Classic Handprints, Vol. II) Tassled drapery swags embellished with an oak-leaf and acorn motif, all neatly tied together with a ribbon detail. Page 219

Neoclassical Toile: Silver Blue and Sky (Classic Handprints, Vol. II) Available in a variety of colorways. Pages 22–23 (Cherry and Wood) and 220–221

Sichuan Border: Indigo (Pergola) A strong architectural pattern on a crackled ground, offset by the delicacy of the undulating leaf pattern. Pages 220–221

Somerby: Cornflower (Petite Prints) Diamonds and pinstripes in a soft colorway make a versatile wallpaper. Pages 222–223

Seed Packet Border: Yellow (New York Botanical Garden: A Visit to the Garden) Antiqued seed packets to energize any garden room. Pages 222–223

Parrot Tulips: White and Multi (Preservation) One can surely understand the tulip mania of the seventeenth century when looking at this print. Page 224

Balkan Weave: White and Blue (Grand Bazaar) A faux needlepoint design transports; available in several colorways. Page 225

Andover Strie: Periwinkle (Classic Essentials) A classic pattern in a muted colorway. Pages 226–227

Kashi Kahn: Peach and Blue (Encore IV, Asian Influence) One of Schumacher's best-selling prints for the past several decades. Pages 226–227

Bordure du Provence: Blue and White (Papiers de France) Pretty paisleys and stripes for a country kitchen or boudoir. Page 228

Gracie Stripe: Sky (Classic Essentials) The tonal quality creates another dimension to the basic stripe. Pages 189 (Cyprus) and 229

Serenade Scroll: Periwinkle (Garden Pleasures) A small-scale all-over scroll; the density of its pattern is offset by the restrained colorway. Page 230

Thorburn's Geranium: Purple on Cream (Victorian) A posey of geraniums dance on a printed moire background. Pages 230–231

Charlot Chevron: Blue (Garden Pleasures) Small-scale chevrons inspired by a woven fabric document. Page 231

"Wallpaper has taken me on many journeys past and present. As a child, I slept in an Edwardian rose garden, dined in the Far East among mandarins, dragons and pagodas, and bathed in steamy tropical splendor. I remember each room vividly and so loved those wallscapes."
—Maude LaFontaine, designer

Diamond Pearl Check: Plum and Metallic (Viewpoint) Golden pearls suspended on an amethyst tool-leathered background, based on a document wallpaper. Page 234

Drape Twist Border: Tan and Ochre (Encore IV) Couture for the walls. Page 235

Jodhpur Border: Purple (India) A lovely, concise border to be paired with Jodhpur Floral. Page 236

Jodhpur Floral: Mocha (India) A floral vine, in an embroidered style, on a coffee ground. Page 236

Acanthus Scroll Border: Gold and Eggplant (Tone on Tone II) A small border on a grand scale: Acanthus leaf and scroll between a rope border. Page 237

Fruited Vine Border: Aubergine (Tone on Tone II) The vibrancy of this color choice on both the fruit and the rope border visually pops off this rich violet background. Page 238

Royal Pinstripe: Plum (Viewpoint) This narrow ribbon is the perfect detail for a royal trimming. Page 239

Napa Valley Fruit Border: Butterscotch (Encore IV) The grape cluster makes this Napa Valley homage a juicy choice for a countertop border in a country kitchen. Page 239

Star and Pearl Border: Plum and Metallic (Viewpoint) Baubles, bangles, and beads for those that want to give the tops of their walls the royal treatment. Page 240

Belter Damasquette: Purple (Victorian) Victorian floral bouquet in a rich aubergine. Pages 240–241

Blackwell: Plum (Hallways) The faux slate treatment of the embedded diamonds is offset by the gentle stencils in this deep purple paper. Page 242

Vernon Textured Floral: Purple and Beige (Textural Classics) Distressed floral on a metallic background: softness and strength in one wallcovering. Page 243

Jaipur Turban Stripe: Plum and Cadet (India) Inspired by striped textiles of India. Page 244

Raphael Arabesque: Brown (Victorian) A floral arabesque vine in a well-balanced coloration; showcases a very sophisticated palette. Pages 244-245

Abingdon Stripe: Wine (Haberdashery) This colorway only emphasizes the boldness and strength of the pattern. Perfect in rooms laden with dark woods. Page 245

"Wallpaper is like a lovely wrapping paper—it's just that it's not as easily removed!"
—Doretta Sperduto, *Metropolitan Home*

Ahmedabad Stripe: Purple (India) An interplay of beige and aubergine, with a hint of garnet, for those bold enough to use the scheme. Pages 189 (in Aqua) and 244–245

Toile Arabesque: Biscuit and Purple (Historic Savannah, Vol. II) Frolicking children in an arabesque frame making music in the garden. Pages 105 (Yellow and Red) and 246–247

Taliesin Frieze Border: Jade and Maize (Frank Lloyd Wright Collection) Architectural border inspired by Frank Lloyd Wright drawings. Pages 248–249

Hadley Stripe: Purple and Green (Stripes & Plaids) A beautiful marriage of a fresh color combination with a fresh pattern. Enlighten a small space or burst a large space wide open. Pages 248–249

Bande Royale: Scarlet (Classic Essentials) The lining of a band box inspired this perennial favorite. Page 252

Tierni Damask: Garnet (Classic Essentials, Damask II Collection) A textured classic red-drenched damask. Page 253

Premier Strie: Scarlet (Classic Essentials) Like a bottle of fine red wine: delicate and bold. Page 253

Windsor Wreath: Gold on Red (Classic Handprints, Vol. II) Laurel wreath leaf on a striped linen-textured background. A handprint. Pages 254–255

Classic Bee: Red (Classic Handprints, Vol. II) This Napoleonic tone poem has bees arranged in military precision. Pure elegance. Page 255

Ming Pavilion: Red (Classic Handprints, Vol. II) Camel-colored chinoserie figures and imagery on a lush red ground create a dramatic display in this handprinted paper. Page 256

Trailing Leaf Border: Red and Green (Mini Motifs) The density of color and pattern in this narrow border packs a worthy design punch. Page 257

Jeffrey's Ferroneric: Red (Victorian) A Victorian representation of an elegant red-on-red damask. Page 257

"The best thing about wallpaper is that it has a romantic quality. Besides the instant visual romance, there is the romance of the paper over time. I grew up in a house which was wallpapered several times over; I would find a corner and peel back each paper to remember what the room was like."
—Scott Salvator, designer

Dominique Stripe: Red (Classic Essentials) This red-on-red stripe achieves an ombre affect, further distinguished by its heavy saturation of color. Page 258

Dutch Garden: Red & Multi (Classic Handprints, Vol. II) A field of large-scale blossoms handprinted against a rich red field. Page 259

Mariana Drape Border: Red (Border Book V) A stunning trompe l'oeil interpretation containing the perfect balance of colors. Page 260

Mille Fleurs: Multi on Red (Mini Motifs) The French joie de vivre translates here into a toss of tiny flowers against a red sky. Pages 260–261

Toscana Braid Border: Rose and Tan (Classic Handprints, Vol. II) A braided pattern of rose and beige simulating a woven ribbon, with architectural beading. Page 261

"Color is the sun and moon of the interior. It can light up your life or create a dark mood."
—Michael R. LaRocca, Michael R. La Rocca Ltd.

Feuillage Ombre: Red (Border Book V) Inspired from a document wallpaper, this is a satisfying print available in a variety of colorways. Pages 262 and 266 (Raspberry)

Cordova Fruited Vine: Aubergine (Cuisine et Salle de Bains) Large-scale fruit and floral toile vine. Page 263

Damask Silk: Red (Vintage Textiles) Stunning tone-on-tone work conceals hidden depths in this paper, and will add intrigue to any room. Page 264

Silk Flower Border: Red (Vintage Textiles) A watercolor study of peonies, dripping with freshness. Page 265

Feuillage Ombre: Raspberry (Classic Essentials) Shown on Page 262 in the red colorway. See also page 266.

Serpentine Damask: Shell (Viewpoint) A suggestion of water-stained silk serves as the perfect backdrop for any sitting room. Page 267

"Wallpaper holds together half the wall surfaces in New York apartments."
—Tom Fleming of Irvine, Fleming, Bell, LLC

Damask Arabesque Cork: Sepia (Designs for Men) A large scale, show-stopping damask handprinted on cork. Pages 270–271

Country House Toile: Black (Country House) A wonderful juxtaposition: a traditional floral motif printed in a bold, modern palette. Page 272

Walton Plaid: Charcoal (Stripes & Plaids) A masculine plaid to evoke Walton Street in the Chelsea area of London, a street laden with antique shops. Page 273

Coca-Cola: Black and Red (Fresh Fashion, Vol. III) It's the real thing: a fun, refreshing wallpaper. Pages 274–275

Botanical Scenic Toile: Onyx (New York Botanical Garden: A Visit to the Garden) A garden tour in toile-like Gotham. Pages 274–275

Gilded Stripe: Coral and Gold (Classic Handprints, Vol. III) Wide-wale gold and copper printed on craft paper. Pages 276–277

Gilded Leaves: Silver Copper (Classic Handprints, Vol. III) Stylized overlapping copper and pewter leaves; this design is a good example of how the metallics appeared in wallpapers in the 1970s. Pages 276–277

"You can almost think of wallpaper like you would clothes, as wallpaper dresses a space."
—Libby Cameron, designer

Losange: Pewter (Designs for Men) Handsome super-chic cut diamonds, printed on a pewter craft. Pages 276–277

Hemba Leopard: Cream (Neutral Collection) This wallpaper never changes its spots, nor should it: a classic. Pages 278–279

Weathervanes: Wheat (Country House) Whimsical weathervanes for the lover of rural antiques. Pages 278–279

Akita: Oatmeal (Texture Collection) Subtle texture, shown to scale within the book; enlarged, it appears behind the designers' quotes in this index. Pages 278–279

Sherbrooke Dog Toile: Bark (Designs for Men) A masculine toile suitable for men's libraries and hunting lodges. Page 280–281

Kumamoto: Sand (Texture Collection) A three-dimensional textured wallcovering sensitively displaying all the neutral shades of decorative grass. Page 279

Tropical Rain: Wheat on Cream (Blue Ribbon) A Chuck Fischer original, shown to scale within the Neutral section, and in greatly reduced scale as the endpapers of this book. Pages 141 (Green on Pale Yellow) and 282–283

> **"When designing a home, think of your wallpaper as you would when assembling the ultimate cocktail party. There are some that you want to be quiet and just look pretty, and others that will take center stage. While others are shy and demure, there are those that scream, 'Look at me . . . I'm the wallpaper!'"**
>
> **—Susan Zises Green, designer**

Leopard Skin: Champagne (Hallways) A medium-scale tone-on-tone leopard. Page 284

Petits Elephants: Ivory (Designs for Men) Wallpaper fit for a raj. Page 284

Crocodilian: Alabaster (Designs for Men) A cushiony tone-on-tone design inspired by the elegant use of crocodile in menswear fashion. Page 285

La Sila Border: Ivory (Surface Impressions) An architectural dental molding, handprinted; use to create grandeur in a room. Pages 284–285

Sichuan Vine: White (Pergola) A delicate interplay of leafs form a subtle backdrop for any room. Pages 286–287

Mataro: Champagne (Surface Impressions) An African-inspired abstract pearlescence stripe. Page 288

Field Stripe: Beige (Encore IV) A classic stripe. Page 288

Wild Card: Ivory (Designs for Men) The playing card motif may seem too playful for some, but the softness of the neutral tone-on-tone makes this design a safe bet. Pages 288–289

Florentine Imberline: Ivory (Neutral Collection) An elegant interplay of an imberline stripe for damask doyennes. This forms the left backdrop on the front matter of this book. Page 290

Bruton Damask: White Pearl (Williamsburg: A Legacy of Style) This signature damask has been in Schumacher's design repertoire for decades, and forms the right backdrop for the front matter of this book. Page 291

> **"Too bad there is no beige in the rainbow."**
>
> **—Bruce Bierman, designer**

ACKNOWLEDGMENTS

Special thanks to the following for making this book possible:

Charles Miers, Publisher, Rizzoli/Universe; Brian McCafferty, Lionize, Inc.; F. Schumacher & Co., specifically Janice Langrall, Corine Sacco, Nick Lomangino, Gerard Wilder, Rose Fiorilli, Katy Muller, and the Schumacher design studio; my editor, Jessica Fuller, and associate publisher, Bonnie Eldon; Sandra L. Baker, Michael Montana, Steven Wargo, Leonard J. Charney, the Wade Maxx Art Gallery; Albert Hadley; Renee Meyers; Nicholas Pentecost; Joan Marcus; Paul Dobrowolski; all of the designers and editors who so generously provided quotes; Bill Evans; and my mom, who always had art supplies around the house and who would encourage me to go draw and paint as soon as I started whining, "I'm bored, and I have nothing to do."

ABOUT THE AUTHOR

Chuck Fischer is one of the most talented and sought-after product designers in America today. Chuck has a Bachelor of Fine Arts from the University of Kansas. For the past sixteen years, he has been painting private commission creations for some of the finest residences in the world. His designs are featured in such house and home companies as Lenox, F. Schumacher & Co., Martex, Braemore, Brunschwig & Fils, and H. George Caspari.

He has been accepted as a visiting artist in Italy this year at the American Academy in Rome, and his work is in the permanent collection of the Cooper-Hewitt Museum. *Wallcoverings* is Chuck's second book.

ABOUT ALBERT HADLEY

Albert Hadley was born in Nashville, Tennessee. After World War II he moved to New York to attend and graduate from The Parsons School of Design. In 1962, he began his legendary association with Mrs. Henry "Sister" Parish II. In 1999, Albert Hadley closed the doors of Parish-Hadley and once again began his own firm, Albert Hadley, Incorporated.

For additional information about F. Schumacher & Co. wallcoverings, or to order, please call 1-800-988-7775.